All About
the Great Lakes

Maureen Dunphy

Indianapolis, Indiana

All About the Great Lakes
Copyright © 2020 by Maureen Dunphy

Published by Blue River Press
Indianapolis, Indiana
www.brpressbooks.com

Distributed by Cardinal Publishers Group
A Tom Doherty Company, Inc.
www.cardinalpub.com

ISBN: 978-1-68157-101-0

LCCN: 2018943505

Cover Design: David Miles
Illustrator: Amber Calderon
Book Design: Dave Reed
Cover Artist: Robert Perrish
Editor: Dani McCormick
Special thanks to the National Museum of the Great Lakes

Printed in the United States of America

10 9 8 7 6 5 4 3 2 1   20 21 22 23 24 25 26 27

Contents

For my dear grandchildren,
Avery Grace and Caden Daly,
who I hope will both enjoy many
Great Lakes adventures
and come to love the lakes.

Introduction

A girl and boy were walking on a beach. They were headed to a lighthouse, but it was far off in the distance. Right now, what was at their bare feet was more interesting. Water flooded over their ankles as waves crashed up on the shore. In one hand, the girl shook together pieces of beach glass she had found glinting in the sand: three clear pieces, one brown, and two of different shades of green. The boy tapped a smooth piece of driftwood on his palm like a drumstick.

They were on a quest for a Petoskey stone, a special fossil. Neither had ever seen one on a beach before, but this was the first time either had visited a Great Lake. The girl's grandma had shown her Petoskey stones from Great Lakes' beaches she kept in a jar with water.

Last night at a bonfire, flames had danced between the children with their families and this Great Lake. While they talked and laughed, the lake breathed in and out with its waves beneath a black sky with more stars than the girl ever imagined.

She had described the fossil to the boy. "It has six-sided sections, like honeycomb, with a dot in the middle of each, like an eye. They're easier to see when they're wet. Dry, they usually just look like plain gray stones," she said. They had made plans to look for one today.

This Great Lake looked bigger than the boy thought it could be. Squinting at the horizon, he could understand how earlier people believed the earth was flat and that the Great Lakes were oceans. When he dove into a big wave, the cold was a welcome relief from the heat, just like at the ocean, but without the salty stickiness left on his skin.

Far out, he could see the speck of a freighter. Nothing else was on the horizon, but the sun was heading toward it, reflecting a path on thousands of waves. "Do you think there are shipwrecks at the bottom of this lake?" the boy asked.

"Maybe. How deep do you think it is?" the girl replied, drawing a ship's sail in the wet sand with a stick.

"I don't know," the boy said. "Deep, though! I wonder if there were ever pirates out there."

The girl wondered how such a huge lake had come to be here and why the Great Lakes even existed. A monarch butterfly drifted by on a breeze off the water.

"Let's run. As far as that boat," the boy suggested, motioning to the boat between them and the lighthouse.

"Wait," the girl said, bending to pick up what had just looked like a gray stone until a wave had rewet it. "Look! Look what I found!"

Chapter 1

Sailing Through the Great Lakes to the Ocean

What is the easiest way to remember the names of the five Great Lakes? Some Michiganders use the word "HOMES" to remember them. Each letter in HOMES is the first letter of one of the lakes: Huron, Ontario, Michigan, Erie, Superior. HOMES does not help sailors figure out which lake they are coming to next, though.

To reach the Atlantic Ocean through the Great Lakes, a boat would also need to be navigated through another seven waterways that connect the lakes. In addition to the five Great Lakes, the route through the Great Lakes Basin includes five rivers, one strait, and one secondary lake. This basin also encompasses all of the other waterways that drain into these dozen major bodies of water. The Great Lakes Basin is the largest freshwater system on earth.

The Great Lakes Basin includes the five Great Lakes (shown) and seven other major bodies of water (not labeled).

In learning about the Great Lakes Basin, many students have had the pleasure of reading the book *Paddle-to-the-Sea*. The book's author imagined a Native American boy living near Nipigon, Ontario in Canada. The boy carves a one-foot-long canoe with a wooden paddler seated in it. After the boy is finished, he names the canoe *Paddle-to-the-Sea*. Then he sets the canoe on a hill to wait for the snow to melt. When it does, he hopes *Paddle-to-the-Sea* will end up in the Nipigon River. The Nipigon River flows into the northernmost point of Lake Superior. As he positions the canoe on the hill, the boy tells the paddler what he learned about the Great Lakes in school:

"[W]hen this snow in our Nipigon country melts, the water flows to that river. The river flows into the Great Lakes, the biggest lakes in the world. They are set like bowls on a gentle slope. The water from our river flows into the top one, drops into the next, and on to the others. Then it makes a river again, a river that flows to the Big Salt Water."

Summer programs allow teens to learn navigation and leadership skills on tall ships on the Great Lakes.

Every summer, many teenagers from the United States and Canada have the adventure on a tall ship. A tall ship is a traditionally-rigged sailing vessel. The number of masts on which the sails are hung and how the sails are rigged determines what kind of tall ship it is. Popular modern tall ship rigs include sailing vessels known as full-rigged ships, barques, barquentines, brigs, brigantines, topsail schooners, and yawls. The teens serve as crewmembers, learning leadership and navigational skills. Several organizations offer different programs of varying lengths and with different sailing routes through the Great Lakes.

If such a sailing adventure through the Great Lakes were planned to depart from the port of call farthest from the Atlantic Ocean, it would set sail from Duluth, Minnesota. In order to get to the Atlantic Ocean from Duluth, the tall ship would travel 2,340 miles! On this journey, the ship would navigate through at least 10 of the 12 major bodies of water in the Great Lakes Basin. In order from West to East, the 12 are: Lake Superior, the St. Marys River, Lake Michigan, the Straits of Mackinac, Lake Huron, the St. Clair River.

Lake St. Clair (a secondary lake), the Detroit River, Lake Erie, the Niagara River, Lake Ontario, and the St. Lawrence River. The St. Marys River drains into Lake Huron, not Lake Michigan. Once the ship got to Lake Huron, if the crew wanted to explore Lake Michigan, they would need to head the ship west through the Straits of Mackinac. Then the ship would need to go back through the Straits to Lake Huron to continue its journey to the ocean.

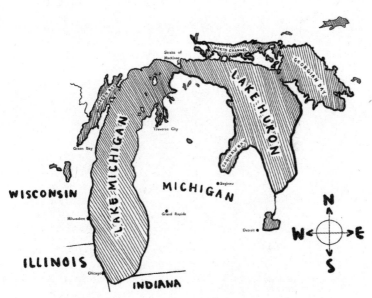

Hydrologists identify only four Great Lakes, one of them being Lake Michigan-Huron.

If the crew attended a class given by a hydrologist—a scientist who studies the waters of the earth—crewmembers would learn something not everyone knows about the Great Lakes. Hydrologists report there are only four Great Lakes! They consider Lake Michigan and Lake Huron two parts of the same lake. This is because the lakes are at the same surface elevation of 577 feet above sea level, as are the Straits of Mackinac that connect them. Lake Michigan-Huron could be considered the largest freshwater lake in the world by surface area. It has a total surface area of over 45,000 square miles, which is significantly larger than Lake Superior.

Paddle-to-the-Sea's journey to the "Big Salt Water" began in a brook that led to the Nipigon River which flows into the Nipigon Bay in Lake Superior, the Great Lake that is superior in many ways.

Lake Superior is one of the largest freshwater lake in the world by volume. It holds three quadrillion gallons of water! That is more than the water in all the other Great Lakes combined. Lake Superior is superior to the other lakes in other ways too. If Lake Michigan and Lake Huron are considered separate lakes, Lake Superior ranks first in size by surface area. Compared to the other Great Lakes, Lake Superior is also the highest, averaging 602 feet above sea level, and the deepest, with an average depth of 483 feet and a deepest point of 1,333 feet. In addition, Lake Superior is the coldest of the Great Lakes, with an average temperature of 40 degrees Fahrenheit, and the cleanest and clearest with underwater visibility of 27 to 75 feet.

Lake Superior may also seem wilder than the other lakes because 68 percent of the land surrounding it is forest. Poor soil and cool weather in this part of the region made it unattractive to farmers. Once the virgin forest was logged in the 19th and 20th centuries, second-growth forest was allowed to grow. Logging is still an important industry here, but all is not forest. Duluth, for instance, is an industrial city.

The St. Marys River flows from Lake Superior into Lake Huron and serves as an international border between the United States and Canada. The Sault Ste. Marie International Bridge rises high up over the St. Marys River and connects Sault Ste. Marie, Michigan to Sault Ste. Marie, Ontario. The French name of these twin cities is pronounced: "Soo-Saint-Marie."

Soon after the tall ship entered this 75-mile-long river and right after it went under the bridge, the river would drop 21 feet through the St. Marys Rapids. The tall ship could not survive these rapids, nor can large freighters. For this reason, the Soo Locks were built here.

The tall ship would need to navigate into the Poe Lock or the MacArthur Lock, where the crew would watch the massive solid steel gates close behind the ship. Then the crewmembers would feel the ship descend as the water level went down with-in the lock. While the water level was changing, they might wave to the tourists watching from the observation platform overlooking the MacArthur Lock. When the depth of the water in the lock matched that outside the gate at the other end, that gate would open. Safely through the drop of the rapids, the tall ship would be free to navigate around several islands and enter Lake Huron.

Before traversing Lake Huron, the crew could choose to navigate west through the Straits of

Lake Michigan is the only Great Lake
entirely within the United States.

— 9 —

Mackinac to explore Lake Michigan. The sand dune featured on the cover of this book is part of Sleeping Bear Dunes located on the eastern shore of Lake Michigan. The dunes' name comes from an Ojibwe legend seeking to explain this natural formation. The legend tells of a mother bear and her two cubs attempting to swim across Lake Michigan in order to escape a forest fire on its western shore. The mother bear made the swim, but her cubs could not. In the story, Sleeping Bear Dunes is the mother bear looking across the water to her cubs: the islands of North and South Manitou.

The Mackinac Bridge, also called the Mightly Mac, is the longest suspension bridge, measured from shore to shore, in the United States and Canada.

Lake Michigan is the only Great Lake entirely in the United States. The international border runs through the other Great Lakes and their connecting waterways, except for the Straits of Mackinac. Lake Michigan is the third largest of the Great Lakes. It stretches 307 miles from north to south and 118 miles across. While its average depth is 279 feet, it is 925 feet at its deepest point. Milwaukee and Chicago are located on Lake Michigan.

The Straits of Mackinac (pronounced Mack-uh-naw) are five miles long. The Mackinac Bridge spans the Straits at the narrowest point of the main strait, connecting the Upper and Lower Peninsulas of Michigan.

From the Mackinac Bridge, people in cars can see three islands to the east in the Straits. The northernmost island is the popular tourist attraction of Mackinac Island, accessed by passenger ferry. No cars are allowed on the island. Visitors and residents of this island get around by horse, carriage, bicycle, and on foot.

Lake Huron contains the Georgian Bay,
once mistaken as a sixth Great Lake.

Lake Huron is the second largest of the Great Lakes by surface area and third largest by volume. It is 183 miles from north to south and 206 miles across. Its average depth is 196 feet, and its deepest point is 750 feet.

As recently as 1815, Lake Huron's very large Georgian Bay was mistaken by Captain William Fitzwilliam Owen to be a sixth Great Lake. This British naval officer and explorer, who surveyed the Upper Canadian Great Lakes, named it Lake Manitoulin. Almost as large as Lake Ontario, it was later determined to be a bay and renamed in honor of King George IV. The eastern side of the Georgian Bay contains the world's largest freshwater archipelago called the 30,000 Islands. At the northern end of Lake Huron, a 100-mile-long island helps create the Georgian Bay. This is Manitoulin Island, the largest freshwater island in the world.

At its southernmost point, Lake Huron drains into the St. Clair River. This river splits into three main branches at the world's largest freshwater delta called the St. Clair Flats. Then it splits again, going around six islands before draining into Lake St. Clair, a secondary lake in the Great Lakes Basin. Lake St. Clair drains into the Detroit River.

As the tall ship entered the Detroit River, it would pass by Belle Isle, the largest city park on an island in the US. Next it would sail under the Ambassador Bridge, spanning the Detroit River between Detroit and Windsor. This bridge is the busiest international border crossing in North America in terms of the number of goods traveling across it. After winding around a number of islands, the Detroit River drains into Lake Erie.

Lake Erie is the shallowest and the smallest of the Great Lakes by volume.

Lake Erie's elevation is 569 feet. Erie is the fourth largest of the Great Lakes by surface area: 241 miles from west to east and 57 miles from north to south. By volume, Lake Erie is the smallest of the lakes. With an average depth of 62 feet, Lake Erie's deepest point is 210 feet. This shallow depth can result in dangerous navigation conditions, particularly in November storms.

In the western basin of Lake Erie, the Pelee archipelago contains 22 islands. The industrial cities of Cleveland and Erie are on the south shores of the lake. Ontario claims the north shore of Lake Erie. Buffalo, New York is at the easternmost end of the lake where it drains into the Niagara River.

Niagara Falls started forming over 12,000 years ago, at the end of the latest Ice Age.

During the Niagara River's length of 36 miles, it drops 326 feet! Over half of this drop happens at the Niagara Falls. Three waterfalls make up the Niagara Falls: The American Falls, 176 feet above the Niagara Gorge into which they fall; the Bridal Falls, which also belong to the US; and the Canadian Horseshoe Falls, which fall 167 feet. Besides their majestic drop, the width of the falls is quite impressive. At their brink, the American Falls are 1,100 feet wide and the Horseshoe Falls are 2,500 feet.

Ontario, the name of both a Canadian province and a Great Lake, may have come from the Iroquois word "skanadario," which translates into "sparkling water." Another origin may be the Wyandot word "Ontarío" meaning "great lake."

What's a tall-ship captain to do? No on-the-spot canal or lock can help with such a drop in elevation. Instead, pleasure boaters and ship captains avoid the Niagara Falls by navigating through Canada's Welland Canal, equipped with eight locks to connect Lake Erie to Lake Ontario.

Notice how similar in size and shape Lake Ontario is to Lake Erie. Lake Ontario is just a little smaller: 193 miles from west to east and 53 miles from north to south. However, Lake Ontario's average depth is 283 feet, with its deepest point at 801 feet. The much deeper Lake Ontario holds almost four times the amount of water as Lake Erie. Lake Ontario is surrounded on its north and west sides and a part of the southwest by Ontario, and New York is on the remainder of its southern shore and at the eastern end. The Ontario cities of Toronto, Mississauga, and Hamilton wrap around Lake Ontario's northwestern end, and Rochester, New York is on its southern shore.

Leaving Lake Ontario, the tall ship would finally head down the St. Lawrence River. All the water from the Great Lakes ultimately drains through this river into the North Atlantic Ocean. According to Environment Canada:

> *"On average, a drop of water which finds its way into Lake Superior from runoff or rainfall . . . takes more than two centuries to travel through the Great Lakes system and . . . the St. Lawrence River to the ocean."*

The Great Lakes Basin ends where the St. Lawrence Basin begins, just before Montreal, Quebec. Before the ship got there, it would navigate around what are known as the Thous-and Islands. This archipelago is made up of almost double the number of islands described by its name. The crew would leave the last of these 1,864 islands in the ship's wake and cruise the rest of the way down the St. Lawrence to the Atlantic Ocean. Just imagine the wonderful memories the crewmembers will have of their journey through the Great Lakes to the "Big Salt Water," the Atlantic Ocean.

Chapter 2
Gift from the Glaciers

Many people use the shapes of the Great Lakes and the "mitten" of Michigan that the lakes form on a map to figure out where other places in the United States or Canada are located. The Great Lakes are so vast that they can even be used this way from space.

The six quadrillion gallons of water in the Great Lakes are easily visible, on a clear day, from space.

However, seeing the Great Lakes from space as clearly as they appear on a map is unusual. These five bodies of water are so massive that they make their own weather. This "lake-effect" weather often includes clouds, so at least some parts of the Great Lakes are usually covered when viewed from space.

Before the Great Lakes existed and affected our weather, weather helped create them. How were the Great Lakes formed? The five majestic Great Lakes have the shapes they have today because of fire and ice, plus some salt and a billion years!

Geologists believe the earth is approximately four and a half billion years old. The Great Lakes are among the youngest natural features on the North American continent. One billion years ago, these five lakes did not exist in any form. What did exist was a 950-mile fracture in the earth that ran from Kansas to where Lake Superior is today. Intense volcanic activity from our planet's core burst up through this Midcontinent Rift. For about 20 million years, during the Precambrian Era, lava flowed from this split. Over time, mountains were created and then eroded. Eventually, from beneath higher land, molten rock began spewing out. The highlands sank and formed the huge rock basin that would someday hold Lake Superior.

Before freshwater flowed through the Great Lakes, two other forms of water played a part.

Marine organisms evolved during the Paleozoic Era, 60 million years ago, when warm shallow seas and tropical jungles covered what is the Great Lakes region today.

After millions of years of heat, the Earth cooled down. For some time, during what is called the Paleozoic Era, a shallow saltwater sea covered the area where the Great Lakes would form. During this era, marine organisms evolved. Over time, coral, shells, and marine-life skeletons accumulated on the bottom of this sea. Eventually compacted by its own weight, this material turned into limestone. Meanwhile, the sea drained and refilled repeatedly, finally leaving behind marshes and areas of limestone bedrock containing many marine fossils.

The large marshes were drained by a system of ancient rivers known as the Laurentian River System. Laurentia is the name of the early continent that became North America and Greenland. The Laurentian River ran from the northern basin of what is now Lake Michigan through the Straits of Mackinac and Lake Huron's basin into the Georgian Bay, then underground to and through Lake Simcoe (a secondary lake in the Great Lakes Basin today), then back underground to the present-day St. Lawrence River, and finally, out to the Atlantic Ocean.

Great tributaries of the St. Laurentian River drained other parts of the marsh. The Huronian River ran from the southern basin of what would become Lake Michigan and across the Lower Peninsula to what is now the Saginaw Bay in Lake Huron. The Erigan River ran where Lake Erie is now and then north and east through where Lake Ontario is today.

The Laurentide Ice Sheet covered the Great Lakes region and most of Canada several times over the Pleistocene epoch, often called the Ice Age.

Then the Earth got very cold. Scientists have theories about why this happened but are not sure. The Great Lakes region and Canada became covered with ice, known as the Laurentide Ice Sheet. For the next 5 million years, the earth went through a series of ice ages. When we talk about "the Ice Age," we are usually referring to the Pleistocene Epoch, the most recent of these ice ages, which took place two million years ago. During this epoch, there were a number of periods where glaciers advanced, meaning they got bigger, and then retreated, growing smaller.

The last of these glacial periods is called the Wisconsin Glacial Stage. The Great Lakes formed at the end of this stage—between 14,000 to 11,000 years ago. The youngest lake to be formed, Lake Erie, took the form it has today only about 12,000 years ago.

Scientists know a lot about the glaciers that helped create the Great Lakes because Antarctica and Greenland are still almost buried by glaciers. Our word "glacier" comes from the Latin word meaning "ice." If you have seen a glacier, you may have been surprised that it looked blue. There are two factors that contribute to a glacier's blue appearance. One is that the weight of a glacier presses the air bubbles out of its ice. In thin ice, white light gets reflected off the air bubbles equally across the color spectrum, so the ice appears white. The second factor contributing to the blueness of a glacier is that the water molecules that make up dense ice are able to absorb the long wavelengths, or the red part, of sunlight.

The short wavelengths, or blue light, is what remains to be scattered throughout the glacier and reflected, making the glacier appear blue.

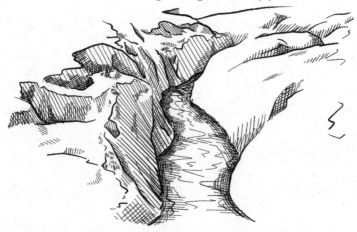

The Greenland glacier is the world's second largest ice sheet. Only the Antarctic ice sheet is larger.

Where did the glaciers come from? Imagine snow starting to fall, continuing to fall, and then not melting because the earth was not warming up fast enough anymore. More snow fell in winters than could melt during summers. The snow piled up, inches becoming feet and feet becoming yards. The increasing weight of this snow piling up pushed the air out of the individual snowflake crystals, which then melted and refroze, creating ice in the place of snow. Eventually, this layer of ice became more than 5,280 feet—more than a mile—deep!

Even more snow fell in the Hudson Bay area. When the snow there got two miles thick, it became too heavy to remain in one place, and, assisted by gravity, started moving southward a few inches a day. When the amount of ice was at its greatest during this period, four million square miles of North America was covered by great ice fields of glaciers.

As these immense glaciers moved, everything in their path was carried along with them, including boulders. Today, some of the gouges made by debris caught beneath the slowly moving glaciers are still visible. The best place on the planet to see such gouged-out paths is at Ohio's Glacial Groove State Memorial on Kelleys Island in Lake Erie. There, deep glacial grooves were carved in the soft limestone bedrock by glacial activity about 18,000 years ago. Workers quarrying limestone discovered these glacial grooves in the 1830s. The exposed glacial grooves measure 430 feet long by 35 feet wide and are up to 15 feet deep. The area was designated as a National Natural Landmark in 1967.

The glacial grooves of Kelleys Island
are a popular tourist destination.

The debris, along with the sharp ice of the glacier itself, scoured the Laurentian riverbeds. This scouring made the riverbeds deeper and wider, ultimately turning them into lake basins. Before the last stage of the most recent ice age left us the five Great Lakes as we know them today—Superior, Michigan, Huron, Erie and Ontario—older versions of these lakes existed. These earlier glacial Great Lakes were different sizes and shapes than today's lakes. They often drained through different waterways because of the moraines of glacial drift—ridges or mounds of boulders, gravel, sand, and clay—that the glaciers left behind.

Other than Lake Superior's basin, which got a hot headstart in a much earlier time, the glacier's scouring movement into the soft limestone bedrock determined the shape of the basin of each of the current Great Lakes. As the earth warmed again and the glaciers melted, the great basins the glaciers had created filled with meltwater. Then, finally, rain contributed water to these new freshwater lakes. The basins filled until the Great Lakes became so very large they could have been seen from space if there had been anyone there to see them.

Chapter 3
Who Called the Great Lakes Region Home First?

When glaciers began to form during the last ice age, no human beings had ever been on the continent of North America. That was about to change. As more of the earth's water got frozen into glaciers, sea levels dropped. In some areas, the seas dropped by 300 feet.

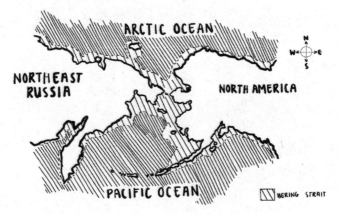

The Bering Land Bridge may be how animals and people crossed from Asia to North America.

When the seas dropped, the land under the Bering Strait was exposed. Today, the Bering Strait is the water between the Chukchi Peninsula in Siberia and the Seward Peninsula of Alaska. Currently, at its narrowest point, this strait is 53 miles wide. The land revealed here when the seas receded is called the Bering Land Bridge. Scientists think this land connected Asia to North America. It may have stretched 600 miles from south to north when the water was lowest. Around 9000 BCE, this land was covered by water again when the glaciers melted and sea levels rose.

A 44,000-year-old Woolly Mammoth excavated from ice in Siberia was exhibited in the St. Petersburg Museum in Russia. Some of her descendants most likely crossed the Bering Land Bridge and grazed in the Great Lakes region as the lakes were forming.

While it existed, the environment of the land bridge was similar to flat, treeless, artic regions called tundra. Grasses, mosses, and lichen would have grown on it.

Such vegetation attracts herbivores, animals that eat plants. Herbivores crossing over the Bering Land Bridge were from some of the 35 families of large mammals that became extinct at the end of the Wisconsin Glacial Stage, between 14,800 BP and 13,000 BP. Mammals that grazed in the Great Lakes region included mammoths, mastodons, musk oxen, great sloths, and giant beavers as large as black bears!

From fossil remains, we can imagine what the carnivore known as a saber-toothed tiger might have looked like.

These large mammals attracted carnivores that preyed upon them. Predators that hunted in the Great Lakes region included saber-toothed tigers, cave lions, giant short-faced bears, and dire wolves.

Anthropologists theorize the first humans lived in Africa or Europe. After migrating into Asia, they eventually came to North America. Since the early 1800s, scientists have theorized that early humans likely followed the predators and their prey onto and across the Bering Land Bridge while hunting. However, recently, another theory has been proposed using sediment cores and DNA analysis. Now researchers are focusing on evidence of migration along the coast, instead of across the land bridge.

Regardless of how they arrived, archeologists call the early humans that appeared on the North American continent Paleo-Indians. "Paleo" means "ancient." Paleo-Indians were the first people who lived in the Great Lakes region. They lived there while the current Great Lakes were forming. Archeologists do not know much about Paleo-Indians, but they know they became extinct about 9,000 years ago.

Archeologists identify different cultures of humans by noticing changes in the appearance of things found at archeological digs. They examine how things were made and for what purposes they appear to have been used. Clues about cultural changes often come from cultural artifacts like arrow tips used for hunting and earthenware pots used for carrying, storing, and cooking food.

After the Paleo-Indians, came Pre-Columbian cultures. These were people who lived in North America before Christopher Columbus explored some islands near the continent. One Pre-Columbian culture was the Archaic people. Divided into Early, Middle, and Late Archaic periods, each period is identified by different cultural artifacts. "Archaic" means "Ancient Ones."

Then came the Woodland people, split into Early, Middle, and Late Woodland periods by what they left behind. The Woodland people existed when deciduous trees began appearing in the evergreen forests. The Late Woodland Native American tribes of the Great Lakes farmed in addition to hunting and gathering.

The people of the Late Archaic period and the people of all three Woodland cultures built large earth mounds for religious, ceremonial, and/or burial purposes. These people, together, are sometimes called Mound Builders. Mound building began in the Great Lakes region, but mounds have been found from the Great Lakes to the Gulf of Mexico and from the Appalachian Mountains to the Mississippi River.

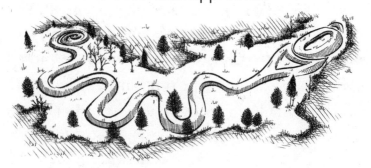

The 1,348-foot Serpent Mound near Peebles, Ohio was most likely built around 321 BCE by the Adena Culture. The descendants of the Adena Culture belong to the Algonquian-speaking native tribes, including the Anishinaabe.

Many earthen mounds were built on top of burial sites in different shapes, including cones, snakes, and birds. The largest mound in North America is in Illinois, measuring 100 feet high and 975 feet long. The greatest number of preserved mounds is south of the Great Lakes in southern Ohio's Hopewell Culture National Historical Park.

The Mound Builders are the ancestors of the Native Americans who Europeans met when they arrived. When Europeans began exploring North America—14,000 years after the Paleo-Indians arrived on the continent—they found a large number of people in the Great Lakes region. Most of these people spoke Anishinaabemowin, an Algonquian language. These people were primarily from three Anishinaabe tribes: Ojibwe (or "Chippewa"), Odawa (or "Ottawa"), and Bodéwademi (Potawatomi). Originally one culture, these tribes belong to the Council of Three Fires, which separated in the year 796 at Michilimackinac.

The Council of Three Fires people are not native to the Great Lakes region. They migrated from the northeast Atlantic coast. The motivation for their migration is fascinating. In *The Mishomis Book: The Voice of the Ojibway*, this story, which was originally recorded on their Midewiwin ("Grand Medicine Society") birch-bark scrolls, is retold.

Mishomis is the Ojibwe word for "grandfather." *The Mishomis Book* contains the stories passed down by Ojibwe grandparents.

In these stories, most of the Anishinaabe on the Atlantic coast decided, before the year 1000, to look for a new home after seven prophets predicted that a light-skinned people would land on their shore, bringing death and destruction. This is called the Seven Fires Prophecy. After a great council meeting, the Ojibwe traveled westward, following a sacred vision. The vision informed them that they would reach their destination when they found "food growing on water."

This journey is known as the Seven Fires Migration because the Anishinaabe made seven stopovers along the way. At each stop, some families stayed behind while others continued on. The migrants moved inland by water, following the St. Lawrence River to the Ottawa River to Lake Nipissing and into the Great Lakes. Their stopping places were a turtle-shaped island in the St. Lawrence River, Niagara Falls, the Detroit

River, Manitoulin Island, Sault Ste. Marie, Spirit Island near Duluth, and Madeline Island.

When the Ojibwe reached Madeline Island, they found *manoomin* ("wild rice" to non-natives), a food that grows on water. The 500-year migration by the Anishinaabe ended in 1490. This was just two years before Christopher Columbus approached a continent that, while new to Europeans, had been home to many generations of families since Paleo-Indians first arrived.

The Ojibwe still harvest *manoomin* in the Great Lakes region.

As they migrated into the Great Lakes region, the Anishinaabe pushed other tribes farther west. Between the crossing of the Bering Land Bridge and the arrival of Europeans, anthropologists estimate 120 different bands of native people occupied the Great Lakes Basin. When

Europeans first arrived, they found about two dozen other tribes living there. These included other Algonquian-language tribes; Iroquois-language tribes including Wyandot (Huron), Erie, and Mohawk; one Siouan-language tribe (Winnebago); and the Meskwaki (Fox).

What happened to these approximately 27 tribes? What happened to the 60,000 to 117,000 native people living in the Great Lakes region in 1700? Native Americans—or First Nations people, as they are called in Canada—had experienced disease and war before meeting Europeans. However, within one century after Europeans arrived, many tribes were decimated by European diseases, for which they had no immunity, or European-style warfare involving guns.

Native people and Europeans thought differently about land. Native people considered land a gift for all to share. Europeans believed in private property, individuals owning land. This difference led to serious misunderstandings. Most of the native people in the Great Lakes region who survived European disease and war were removed from the land on which their ancestors had lived. They were forced to relocate to Indian reservations in the US or Indian reserves in Canada.

Today, the Council of Three Fires still shares the Anishinaabe language and culture. For generations, since 1490, they have harvested the grass called *manoomin* from the northern Great Lakes. *Manoomin* is the Ojibwe's sacred diet staple. *Manoomin* is the prophesized "food growing on water."

Chapter 4

When the Great Lakes Were in New France

The capture of Constantinople in 1453 cut off the overland trade route to China, India, and the Southeast Asian islands, known as the Silk Road. This began an age of exploration, as European countries tried to find a way to get to The East by sailing west.

"Wanted: Northwest passage by water to get to profitable luxury goods in the Far East." Merchants of five European countries in the sixteenth century could have posted this notice. European exploration of the Great Lakes began with Europeans' desire for luxuries and the profits that came with selling them. Chinese silk, Indian cotton, and spices including black pepper, cinnamon, cloves, and nutmeg, were not found in Europe. Instead, European merchants traded European goods with merchants in China, India, and Southeast Asian islands for them. Before the end of the sixteenth century, the only routes from Europe to these places were by land. Merchants imagined how much easier it would be to transport goods by ship instead of by camel caravan across the Middle East. In 1522, France joined Spain, England, the Dutch Republic, and Portugal in trying to find a water route west to Asia.

Christopher Columbus, the Italian explorer, had sailed for Spain in 1492, hoping to find a northwest passage. Columbus did not find one, never set foot on North America, nor did he discover any new lands, but he did cross the Atlantic.

In 1960, explorer Helge Ingstad discovered the remains of a human settlement on the island of Newfoundland in Canada. Norwegian archeologist Dr. Anne Stine Ingstad led an international team of archaeologists in excavating the settlement, which included sod houses, a forge, cooking pits, and boathouses. The excavation of this settlement from the year 1000 provided proof that other Europeans—Vikings from Scandinavia— had made it to the continent of North America 500 years before Christopher Columbus explored its already inhabited offshore islands.

In 1497, another Italian, Giovanni Caboto, known as John Cabot, had sailed for the English. He became the first European since the Vikings to reach North America. He landed on Newfoundland, which was already inhabited by native people. Nonetheless, he claimed the island for England.

The French explored North America via the St. Lawrence River. Native Americans told them that at the head of the river were the Great Seas, their name for the Great Lakes. In 1534, France began claiming land in the region and soon had more territory in North America than Britain and Spain combined.

The land that would eventually become Quebec, Ontario, and Michigan was only part of New France. The five colonies that made up New France were Canada, Hudson's Bay, Acadie, Plaisance (on what is now the island of Newfoundland), and Louisiane. At the time, Louisiane included the Mississippi River Basin and stretched from the Great Lakes in the North to the Gulf of Mexico in the South, and from the Appalachian Mountains in the East to the Rocky Mountains in the West.

When the French got to the Great Lakes, they survived by hunting, trapping, and trading with Native Americans. They traded knives, guns, tools, beads, and liquor for what they needed and for furs they could sell. When the French did not discover a northwest passage through the Great Lakes, their plans changed. They focused on claiming more land and killing beavers for their fur. In addition, souls became a prize, as Jesuit missionaries arrived to convert native people to Catholicism. Where did this shift occur in France's exploration of the Great Lakes region? It is not hard to spot the shift in this 240 years of French exploration and colonization.

Giovanni de Verrazano (1485 – 1528) was an Italian navigator sailing for the French. In 1523, he explored the North American coast from the Carolinas to Newfoundland. He charted the Atlantic coast but did not discover a passage west to the East.

Jacques Cartier (1491 – 1557) explored the west coast of Newfoundland, discovered Prince Edward Island, and sailed through the Gulf of St. Lawrence into the St. Lawrence River in 1534. Cartier was the first European to make contact with the Hurons. He claimed the St. Lawrence River and its shores for France and was the first European to map the Gulf of St. Lawrence.

Samuel de Champlain (1574 – 1635) came to North America in 1604 and built the Fort of Quebec, founding Quebec City, which was to be a way station between France and China once he found the Northwest Passage. He paddled from the French River out into the Georgian Bay. Called the "Father of New France," Champlain served as its second governor. He created the 1613 and 1632 maps of New France.

Étienne Brûlé (1592 – 1633) arrived with Champlain on his 1608 trip. In 1610, Champlain sent him into the wilderness to learn about the native people and their lands. With his companion

The French first claimed land on the continent now known as North America in 1534. By 1712, New France had grown from one colony to five, and the population had increased to about 70,000 people by the mid-1700s.

Grenolle, Brûlé was the first European to travel up the St. Marys River.

Jean Nicolet (1598 – 1642) arrived in 1618 and was the first European to paddle through the Straits of Mackinac and into Lake Michigan. He lived with Algonquian-language tribes until the English captured the St. Lawrence colony in 1629. Then he moved inland among the Huron. His 1634 – 1635 expedition was to the land of the Winnebago, now Wisconsin, to claim more land for New France. He did not find the Northwest Passage, but he did notice how plentiful beavers were in the Great Lakes region and helped expand the profitable fur trade.

René-Robert Cavelier, Sieur de La Salle (1643 – 1687) first arrived in 1666. In 1679, La Salle built the ship *Le Griffon*. Launched in the Niagara River, it was the first sailing vessel on the Great Lakes. La Salle sailed to the western shore of Lake Michigan, collected furs, and established a French presence. From Green Bay, La Salle sent *Le Griffon* back loaded with furs toward Niagara while he explored farther westward.

Father Jacques Marquette (1637 – 1675) arrived in Quebec in 1666 as a missionary. With

A statue of Father Jacques Marquette, in front of Fort Mackinac on Mackinac Island, memorializes the Jesuit priest and Great Lakes explorer.

Father Claude Dablon, Marquette founded the mission of Sault Sainte-Marie. The Soo area became the first European-established city in the Midwest. With Louis Jolliet (1645 – 1700), born in New France, Marquette was the first European to explore the Great Lakes to the Mississippi River.

Daniel Greysolon, Sieur du Lhut ("Duluth") (circa 1639 – 1710) was sent to Montreal in 1674 by Louis XIV to command the French marines and expand French control of North America. In 1678, Duluth led the first French expedition to Lake Superior.

Father Louis Hennepin (1626 – 1704) accompanied La Salle to New France in 1675. After serving a number of churches, Hennepin accompanied La Salle to Niagara Falls, on his *Le Griffon* voyage, and in his exploration of the Mississippi River.

Antoine de la Mothe Cadillac (1658 – 1730) arrived in 1683 as a soldier to fight the Iroquois. He served as the commander of the Michilimackinac frontier post from 1694 to 1697. In 1701, Cadillac selected the place on the Detroit River to build Fort Pontchartrain, founding Detroit.

The French pushed farther into the Great Lakes region, claiming more land and expanding the fur trade. Without the birch-bark canoe, they would not have been able to explore the region,

Birch bark canoes were the best method of transportation
for both native people and explorers in the Great Lakes region.
Birch bark canoes were lightweight, sturdy,
waterproof, and easy to repair.

take control of the resources they found there, or,
in the case of furs, get them to market.

The French created alliances with both
Algonquian-speaking tribes and the Iroquoian-
speaking Huron, who were able to hunt and
trap at commercial levels and were considered
partners in the French fur trade.

Before Europeans arrived, over ten million
beavers lived in the Great Lakes. A process of
felting beaver fur by boiling it was developed in
Europe. The resulting material was made into top
hats called "beavers," which were in fashion from
1625 to the 1800s across Europe.

This European fashion caused war to develop
in the Great Lakes region. The French and Iroquois

Wars (1640 – 1698), also called The Beaver Wars, were fought throughout the St. Lawrence River valley and lower Great Lakes region. The Iroquois Confederacy, a confederation of five Iroquoian-speaking tribes, armed by Dutch and English allies, fought Algonquian-speaking tribes and Hurons, allied with the French. The Iroquois had depleted the beaver population in their St. Lawrence River area and fought for access to trap beavers on other tribes' lands. During this half century of conflicts, the Iroquois destroyed the Huron, Neutral, Erie, Susquehannock, and Shawnee nations. The Beaver Wars ended with the 1701 Great Peace of Montreal treaty between New France and 40 First Nations.

Nonetheless, conflict over land continued between the British, Dutch, French, and Native American tribes. The French and Indian War (1754 – 1763), fought between New France and the colonies of British America, was part of the global Seven Years' War. The French and Indian War ended with the 1763 Treaty of Paris. All of New France went to Great Britain and Spain.

All the Great Lakes went to Great Britain, but not for long.

The American Revolutionary War, beginning in 1775, ended with the 1783 Treaty of Paris, which gave the new United States a northern border of the Great Lakes, among other gains in territory. In the War of 1812, the British would fight the Americans for control of Lake Erie and Lake Ontario. The Battle of Lake Erie would be a turning point in that war. It was also the first time in history a British navy squadron was defeated.

This war was brewing at the start of the nineteenth century. The North American beaver was almost extinct. Some Native Americans had embraced Christianity. One thing had not changed, however. Regardless who controlled the Great Lakes—the French, British, or Americans—they sought to profit from the abundance of riches found there.

Chapter 5
Riches Galore

When European immigrants settled in the Great Lakes region, they took control of the plentiful resources the area had provided Native Americans. These resources included fish, furs, trees, and minerals. In addition to using these resources for themselves, some settlers aimed to get richer by selling these natural resources.

The waterways of the Great Lakes Basin made these plans easier to carry out. Much land surrounding the Great Lakes was covered in dense forest or swamp. The waterways served as highways to get to the resources in the region and then turn those resources into wealth by shipping them to market.

One of the most important resources in the Great Lakes was fish. Native Americans only caught fish for eating, and it was a major part of their diet. Because their survival depended on it, they aimed to catch as many fish as they needed in the shortest period. Gill nets were set up in the water, and dip nets were used from canoes. Fish could be speared at night or trapped in fish traps made with rocks that took advantage of the current.

Tribes from all over traveled to Sault Ste. Marie to catch whitefish in the St. Marys Rapids. Once caught, the fish were smoked and dried. Trout and sturgeon were speared through the ice in winter. In winter, fish could be frozen. Even suckers, catfish, and sunfish were eaten. One way the Anishinaabe cooked fish was to pack it in clay and bury it in the coals of a fire for several hours.

When the Europeans arrived, 150 native species of fish swam in the Great Lakes, including salmon, trout, whitefish, carp, perch, and walleye. All these species are still caught today. But, back then, even lake sturgeon were plentiful.

The lake sturgeon is a prehistoric freshwater fish. They spawn in rivers, live near lakeshores, and feed along lake bottoms. They grow slowly over their lifetimes of 55 to 150 years. Lake sturgeon can grow to be eight feet long and weigh nearly 300 pounds. Their abundant eggs, similar to caviar, are eaten as a delicacy. Native Americans depended on this fish as an important food source, particularly after long winters. They used every part of each one of these huge fish they caught.

Today, lake sturgeon are listed
as either threatened or endangered by
19 of the 20 states in which they are native.

When commercial fishermen took over the lakes, they initially slaughtered lake sturgeon because these big fish destroyed nets used to catch other species. Around 1850, when the fishermen realized the economic value of the fish, they increased their annual catches of lake sturgeon to an average of four million tons.

In the 1900s, the lake sturgeon population decreased. This was not just a result of overfishing. New dams built in Great Lakes waterways prevented the fish from getting to their river spawning grounds to lay their eggs. Other spawning grounds were destroyed by changes in rivers due to logging, farming, and industrial pollution. Today, the lake sturgeon is an endangered species.

Native Americans trapped animals in the region and used their fur to provide warmth as outerwear, for blankets, and to create shelter. When the European explorers arrived, they traded goods for furs to trim fashionable European clothing. Then beaver top hats became very popular. By the 1830s, when silk replaced fur in making the hats, the fur trade began to steeply

Beaver hats were made by shaving the beaver furs and then boiling that fur into a felted material.

decline. The North American beaver was brought back from near extinction. Today, fur used for fashion comes from animals raised on fur farms.

The North American beaver almost became extinct by trapping during the fur trading years.

For centuries, some Native American tribes had been mining copper to use in ornaments, tools, and weapons, and to trade with other tribes. Copper was valued as a symbol of wealth and position and was believed to have supernatural powers. In the western Upper Peninsula of Michigan copper can be found as pure copper metal. Other places, it is found in copper ore, from which the metal must be removed.

When Michigan's Upper Peninsula and Isle Royale were open to miners, copper mining became an important Great Lakes industry in the nineteenth and into the twentieth century. Historically, silver, gold, iron, and zinc mines also operated on the north shore of Lake Superior.

The Ontonagon Copper Boulder was a 3,708-pounds of pure copper near Lake Superior that Native Americans had worshipped. Removed by a Detroit hardware merchant, it was seized by the U.S. War Department and is on display today at the Smithsonian National Museum of Natural History.

While mining continues to be important in the Great Lakes region, iron ore, limestone, sand, and gravel are the primary mining products today. Iron ore is a rock from which metallic iron can be removed. In 2011, mines in Minnesota and Michigan produced 99% of the usable iron ore produced in the United States. Iron ore is used to make pig iron, one of the materials used in making steel.

When European settlement began in the Great Lakes area, forests covered much of the land around the Great Lakes Basin waterways. Settlers cleared trees for farming. Loggers cut trees to

From 1860 to 1900, pine lumbering was a huge industry. Particularly in Michigan, white pines grew as tall as 175 feet high with trunks that were eight feet in diameter.

produce the lumber needed for building houses, barns, city buildings, and ships. The ships moved the lumber and other goods to where they were needed and would be purchased. In the last 150 years, nearly all of the forests around the Great Lakes have been cut at least once, and 60 percent of the forestland has been lost in the development of farms and cities.

Native Americans took advantage of the large number of maple trees in the woodlands of the Great Lakes. They tapped these trees, hanging containers below the hole created in the tree

Ojibwe people tapped maple tree for sap with a sumac peg.

trunks to collect the sap that flowed out. When the sap was boiled, it turned into maple syrup.

Much maple syrup is commercially produced in the Great Lakes region today. Quebec is the largest producer in the world, and Ontario is third. In the United States, Wisconsin, Pennsylvania, Ohio, and Michigan rank in the top 10 maple syrup producers.

Most often, the phrase "renewable resource" is used in talking about renewable energy resources, like wind, sunlight, geothermal heat, and others. Maple sap is a very good example of a renewable natural resource. Maple trees do not need to be destroyed in order for sap to be collected and maple syrup made. People can collect the sap that a maple tree produces this year, and the tree will make more sap that can be collected next year. Maple syrup can be made from the sap of maple trees every year without harming the tree.

The renewability of other "renewable" natural resources tends to be more conditional. Today, if fish populations are managed carefully so that as many fish eggs are laid and hatched as adult fish are caught, fish are considered a renewable natural resource. If a forest is managed for sustainable wood production, so that as many trees are planted as are cut, timber is considered a renewable natural resource. If species of animals that are killed for their fur are protected so that as many young offspring survive as are killed, their fur is considered a renewable natural resource.

An over-harvesting of fish, timber, and fur-bearing animals in the Great Lakes region by the first European immigrants depleted these potentially renewable natural resources. Today, the descendants of those and later immigrants understand how practicing conservation protects the future of the earth as well as these important natural resources. Conservation of natural resources today will positively impact the quality of life for future generations.

Chapter 6
<u>Danger!</u>

Great Lakes shipping expanded in order to move the area's natural resources, and goods made from them, from one place to another. More ships sailing on the lakes meant more wealth, but also involved danger. The possibility of a shipwreck was one of these dangers.

Many ships that sank in the Great Lakes have never been found. The Great Lakes Shipwreck Museum estimates that approximately 6,000 ships and 30,000 lives have been lost in the Great Lakes in the last 340 years. Historian Mark Thompson, author of *Graveyard of the Lakes*, believes the number of shipwrecks on the Great Lakes may be more than 25,000.

We know little about what happened to the first ship that disappeared in the Great Lakes. In January 1679, the French explorer René-Robert Cavelier, known as La Salle from his title Sieur de La Salle, started building a ship in Seneca territory near Cayuga Creek. With a crew, he built a 30 to 40-foot, 45-ton, seven-cannon ship bearing several square sails.

LaSalle's ship, *Le Griffon*, the first full-size ship on the Great Lakes, was launched in 1679 from the Niagara River.

The ship was christened *Le Griffon*. A carved griffon served as the ship's figurehead. A griffon is a mythical creature with the body, back legs, and tail of a lion and the head, wings, and talons of an eagle, a combination of the king of beasts and the king of birds. In Greek mythology, the griffon symbolized strength, courage, and leadership. The captain and crew of *Le Griffon* would need those qualities to make it to the western shore of Lake Michigan, where La Salle planned to collect furs and establish a French presence.

On August 7th, La Salle, the missionary Father Louis Hennepin, and a crew of 32 other men set sail. Cayuga Creek drains into the Buffalo River, which in turn drains into the Niagara River above the Niagara Falls. The ship had to be towed, so it would not get caught in the river's current leading to the Falls. From the Niagara, *Le Griffon* entered Lake Erie, the first sailing vessel on the Great Lakes.

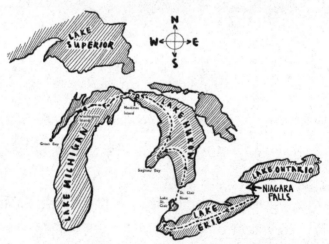

La Salle sailed through three Great Lakes to Green Bay and then disappeared on his way back.

The ship sailed through the uncharted waters of three Great Lakes. The crew faced several challenges on the journey. They nearly hit the sand spit of Long Point that sticks out a mile and a half from Lake Erie's northern shore. They had trouble finding a channel large enough for the ship to get through at the delta between the lake they named Lake St. Clair and the St. Clair River. They fought a gale on Lake Huron.

Le Griffon made it to Green Bay on September 2nd. La Salle loaded the ship with furs, and 16 days later, it headed back toward Niagara without La Salle and half the crew. The ship was never seen again. Theories about its disappearance include that it encountered a violent storm or the ship's pilot committed an act of sabotage.

Shipwreck divers joke that *Le Griffon* is "the most searched for and the most found ship" in the Great Lakes. In one 15-year-period, beginning in 2002, 17 false alarms of *Le Griffon* being found were investigated by a maritime archaeologist for the state of Michigan.

Almost 300 years after *Le Griffon* disappeared, the SS *Edmund Fitzgerald* sank. We know a lot about this most recent major shipwreck on the Great Lakes, but not everything. The *Edmund Fitzgerald* was a 729-foot-long American Great Lakes freighter. The ship had been making trips on Lake Superior for 17 years. On November 9, 1975, it left Superior, Wisconsin carrying a full load of iron ore pellets and heading for a steel mill on Zug Island in the Detroit River.

When it sank in 1975, the *SS Edmund Fitzgerald* was the largest "laker," the name for the large cargo vessels on the Great Lakes, ever built.

Before it entered the St. Marys River on November 10th, a November gale struck. Hurricane-force winds and 35-foot-high waves battered the freighter. The captain's last message to a freighter it had been traveling near was "We are holding our own."

The freighter's entire crew of 29 went down with it. No bodies have ever been found. The *Edmund Fitzgerald* is the largest ship to have ever sunk on any of the Great Lakes. US Navy divers found the wreck four days after it sank in Canadian waters, north of Whitefish Point about 17 miles from Whitefish Bay. The exact cause of the sinking is unknown.

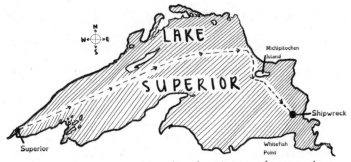

The *Edmund Fitzgerald* sank only minutes after assuring another ship via radio that they were "holding their own."

A 1976 hit song by Canadian singer-songwriter Gordon Lightfoot, entitled "The Wreck of the Edmund Fitzgerald," tells the story of the tragedy, ending with these lines:

The legend lives on from the Chippewa on down
Of the big lake they call Gitche Gumee.
"Superior," they said, "never gives up her dead
When the gales of November come early."

Lightfoot's lyrics contain two names that may puzzle some people. "Chippewa" was the French name for the Ojibwe people and is still used by some Americans. In Canada, Ojibwe is more commonly used to describe the people who call themselves Anishinaabe. "*Gitche Gumee*" is Henry Wadsworth Longfellow's attempt to spell an Anishinaabe word in his 1855 poem "The Song of Hiawatha." Meaning "Big Sea," it refers to Lake Superior, and would more likely be spelled *Kitchi-Gami* today.

Besides 35-foot waves, other maritime dangers were present on the Great Lakes. Great Lakes pirates stole cargos of furs or timber. Sometimes, they stole entire ships.

Only one man is known to have been formally charged with piracy on the Great Lakes. That man was Dan Seavey, according to Chris Gillcrist, Executive Director of the National Museum of the Great Lakes in Toledo, Ohio. "Roaring Dan," as Seavey was nicknamed, put up fake port lights, so captains thought their ships were entering a safe harbor. Instead, they crashed on shoreline rocks.

Once a ship had crashed, Seavey's crew would board the ship and steal its cargo.

One time, in 1908, Seavey stole a cargo ship from Grand Haven, Michigan. The 40-foot schooner, the *Nellie Johnson*, was carrying cedar posts. Authorities chased him by boat the entire way across Lake Michigan to Chicago. After being unable to sell the cedar posts in Chicago, Seavey was arrested near his Michigan home.

The waves and wind of a gale can still make navigating the Great Lakes dangerous. But, in addition to not having to fear pirate raids these days, other things have changed over the years to make navigating the Great Lakes easier.

Chapter 7
Great Lakes Basin, Version 2.0

The Great Lakes Basin has changed significantly since French explorers paddled through it. When ships first sailed the Great Lakes, captains navigated cautiously, staying close to shore by day and anchoring at night. When shipping on the Great Lakes expanded, changes were needed to make the lakes safer and transportation of goods by ship easier.

Lighthouses, lightships, beacons, buoys, foghorns, bells, and radio signals are all used on the Great Lakes. Such aids help ships avoid the dangers of shoreline rocks, underwater shoals, and islands. They also help make navigation easier in severe weather.

The National Park Service reported the Great Lakes had over 400 standing lighthouses in 2013. Almost 90 percent of them were currently aiding navigation. Just 280 years before this report, not one lighthouse beamed light out over the more than 94,000 square miles of the Great Lakes' watery wilderness.

First lit in 1734, the Louisbourg Lighthouse aided sailors on the Atlantic Ocean bound for the St. Lawrence River. It was the first lighthouse built in Canada and the second lighthouse built on the coast of North America. Located at the mouth of the Gulf of St. Lawrence, the Louisbourg Light shone out on the North Atlantic Ocean from Cape Breton Island. This lighthouse showed sailors where to safely enter the gulf. The 54-foot tower was destroyed two years after it was built when its wooden lantern caught fire. Many other lighthouses exist on this island today, but the Louisbourg Light, rebuilt three times, is still active.

The first lighthouse within the Great Lakes Basin was the Fort Niagara Light, which began operating in 1782. Located on the Niagara River near the south shore of Lake Ontario in New York State, it is inactive today. A modern beacon replaced it so that trees blocking its light did not have to be removed.

Mississauga Point Light, the first lighthouse built on the shore of a Great Lake, was built in 1804 on Lake Ontario at the west side of the mouth of the Niagara River. During the War of 1812, it was removed to make room for Fort Mississauga. The slab on which it was built is all that remains.

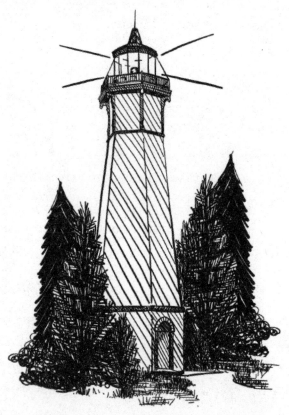

The first keeper of the Toronto Islands' Gibraltar Point Lighthouse was murdered in 1815 and is now a part of the lighthouse's legend.

The Gibraltar Point Lighthouse is on the Toronto Islands in Lake Ontario. Built in 1808, it is the oldest existing lighthouse on the Great Lakes. The Toronto Islands are sandy islands that have shifted over time. Today, the lake can no longer be seen from the base of this lighthouse.

Occasionally, however, people claim to see the light of this inactive lighthouse lit. Its first lighthouse keeper was a bootlegger, who added water to his products. One evening in 1815, he sold liquor to soldiers from the nearby fort. When they attempted to drink it later, it was frozen, which showed it contained a lot of water because alcohol has a lower freezing point than water. They returned to the lighthouse to confront the keeper.

Bloodstains were later found on the lighthouse's wooden steps, and nothing was ever seen of the keeper again. Some people believe when the lighthouse appears to be lit, the lighthouse keeper's ghost has returned. Many other lighthouses, including some of the 144 Great Lakes lighthouses on the US National Register of Historic Places, have interesting stories connected to them too.

Lighthouses were not built on all the Great Lakes at the same time. The first American lighthouses on the Great Lakes were established on Lake Erie at Buffalo, New York and Presque Isle, Pennsylvania in 1818. Marblehead Lighthouse in Marblehead, Ohio, also on Lake Erie, began operation in 1822. Marblehead is the oldest lighthouse in continuous operation on the Great Lakes and continues to help sailors safely navigate past the rocky shores of the Marblehead Peninsula.

The first lighthouse on Lake Huron was the Fort Gratiot Lighthouse, built in 1829 where Lake Huron drains into the St. Clair River. The oldest lighthouse on Lake Michigan is the Pottawatomie Lighthouse, first lit in 1836 on Rock Island in Door County, Wisconsin. Whitefish Point Light, a lighthouse built in 1849 on the Upper Peninsula of Michigan, is the oldest operating lighthouse on Lake Superior.

Lighthouses and other warning systems made navigation safer on the Great Lakes. What happened when trouble did develop out on the water? In the beginning, lighthouse keepers and other volunteers made rescues. The US Life-Saving Service began in 1848. In 1915, it merged with the Revenue Cutter Service (the same government agency that pursued Pirate Seavey across Lake Michigan) to form the US Coast Guard. Canada first had the Department of Marine and Fisheries and then the Department of Transport until the Canadian Coast Guard was formed in 1962.

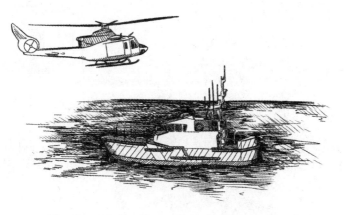

The Great Lakes Coast Guard performs search and rescue operations to keep sailors safe.

Building navigational aids and creating rescue agencies helped make the Great Lakes safer, but engineers had ideas of how navigation on the lakes could be made easier in other ways. To navigate cargo ships from the westernmost point of Lake Superior through the Great Lakes to the Atlantic Ocean became the goal.

Dangerous rapids and waterfalls throughout the Great Lakes Basin prevented such navigation without changes being made. In order to get the maximum commercial value from the lakes, it took many people using their brains and many others using their brawn. Intense human effort

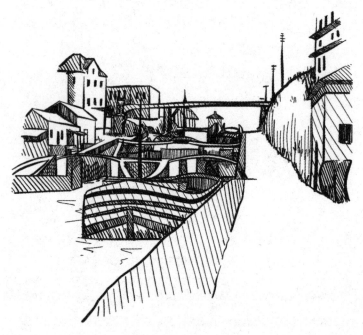

Historically, towpaths along the side of a canal allowed horses or mules to tow barges through the canal, instead of over land. This towpath is along the historic Erie Canal locks at Lockport, NY shown here in the 1890s.

was applied to designing and building canals, locks, and dams throughout the basin.

A combined length of about 1,200 miles of canals touches the Great Lakes, although not all canals are still used. The three best-known canals are the Erie Canal, the Welland Canal, and the St. Marys Falls Canal.

The Erie Canal connects Lake Erie to the Hudson River. It took 10 years to build this 363-mile canal. Because of it, after 1825, ships had access to the Atlantic Ocean without the obstacles of the Niagara Falls or Quebec's Lachine Rapids on the St. Lawrence River. Many Irish immigrants helped dig this canal with picks and shovels. The canal was 40 feet across and initially, five feet deep. One man could dig about a 16-foot length in one week.

The Welland Canal was Canada's solution to the Niagara Falls. Begun the year the Erie Canal opened, the first Welland Canal opened to boats in 1829. Today, the Welland Canal is a 27-mile-long, eight-lock canal between Port Colborne on Lake Erie and Port Weller on Lake Ontario.

The St. Marys Falls Canal contains the Soo Locks and makes the 21-foot drop of the St. Marys River navigable. The first lock in the St. Marys Falls Canal was opened on the Canadian side of the river in 1855. It is a small lock now used for recreational boats. Four American locks handle larger boats and freighters. Every year, approximately 4,500 ships carrying about 80 million tons of cargo—including coal, wheat, limestone, and iron ore—go through the Soo Locks in the 42 weeks that they operate.

The Soo Locks are five locks built on 750,000 acres between the twin cities of Sault Ste. Marie, Michigan and Sault Ste. Marie, Ontario. These locks allow boats to navigate between Lake Superior and the other Great Lakes.

An annual challenge is to prevent the waterways freezing. The challenge begins in January on the northern Great Lakes. The Soo Locks close for 10 weeks of maintenance while the weather is the severest. Before the locks close, icebreakers break the ice to allow ships to make the season's last trip.

The United States Coast Guard Cutter *Mackinaw*, a 240-foot icebreaker, breaking up the January ice.

On the St. Lawrence River between Iroquois, Ontario and Montreal, Quebec, a series of seven locks makes the 243-foot drop between Lake Ontario and the lower St. Lawrence navigable.

Once canals and locks removed the challenges of waterfalls and rapids, the problem of bigger ships being unable to navigate through shallow natural waterways remained to be solved.

Dredging removes rock, sand, gravel, mud, and clay from the bottom of waterways to make them deeper. Dredging has allowed larger ships to navigate through the St. Marys River, the St. Clair Flats channels, and the Detroit River.

At least 12,000 dams are located in the Great Lakes Basin. Three major dams are part of the St. Lawrence Power Project. The Iroquois Dam, the Moses-Saunders Power Dam, and Long Sault Dam help regulate the river's water levels, providing a dependable flow for hydropower.

The St. Lawrence Seaway was a joint project built between 1954 and 1959 by the United States and Canada. The Seaway opened the Great Lakes to ocean-going vessels. Besides creating the hydropower dams, the Seaway project included building canals, constructing locks, and dredging channels. In addition, 6,500 people and 530 buildings were moved. Other buildings, farms, seven villages, and three hamlets were destroyed.

People's dreams, ingenuity, and effort have made many changes to the Great Lakes Basin. Once the St. Lawrence Seaway was completed, a ship could leave Duluth on Lake Superior and travel the 2,340 miles through the chain of the Great Lakes and their connecting waterways, down the St. Lawrence, and out into the Atlantic Ocean. The Great Lakes were connected to the rest of the world, for better or for worse.

Chapter 8
Great Challenges for the Great Lakes

Once the St. Lawrence Seaway was completed, ocean-going vessels were able to travel from all Great Lakes waterways out into the Atlantic Ocean. Of course, ships from all over the world also entered what the French had called Les Mers Douce, or "The Sweetwater Seas." "Sweet" is another way to say "not salty," meaning freshwater. The "sweet" water of the Great Lakes was about to become not so fresh.

Almost exactly ten years after US President Eisenhower and Canada's Queen Elizabeth II ceremoniously opened the St. Lawrence Seaway on June 27, 1959, Lake Erie caught on fire. More precisely, an oil slick on the Cuyahoga River, which flows into Lake Erie, caught fire on June 22, 1969. By then, this river was polluted from decades of industrial waste, like most of the Great Lakes waterways.

In 1952, seventeen years before the fire that provoked environmental action, a fire tug fought the flames of an earlier fire on the Cuyahoga River near downtown Cleveland.

Six major cities are located on the Great Lakes: Milwaukee, Wisconsin; Chicago, Illinois; Detroit, Michigan; Cleveland, Ohio; Buffalo, New York; and Toronto, Ontario. In addition to Duluth, Minnesota, a number of smaller industrial cities line the lakes' shores including Gary, Indiana; Toledo, Ohio; Erie, Pennsylvania; Rochester, New York; Hamilton, Ontario; and Mississauga, Ontario. These cities and their industries have brought wealth to the region, but they have also brought pollution to the Great Lakes.

After the 1969 fire on the water, a number of new water pollution control programs were put in place. These programs included the Clean Water Act and the Great Lakes Water Quality Agreement. This is also when the federal Environmental Protection Agency (EPA) was created.

The RV *Lake Guardian* is the largest Great Lakes' research and monitoring vessel owned by the US Environmental Protection Agency.

The huge iron ore deposits around Lake Superior are located far north from the coal deposits needed to turn iron into steel. The solution was to ship the iron ore to ports on the southern Great Lakes that were closer to the coal mines of Illinois, Indiana, Ohio, and Pennsylvania. Large steel mills were built in Chicago, Gary, Cleveland, Buffalo, and Michigan to take in iron ore and coal and from which to produce and ship out steel.

Mining operations and steel mills discharged their industrial waste into the lakes. After the fire at Lake Erie, environmentalists, scientists, and politicians worked toward enacting strict regulations to control industrial water pollution.

In a 2015 issue of the journal *Ecological Applications* (Vol.25, No.3), the Great Lakes Environmental Assessment and Mapping

Henry Ford's River Rouge automobile plant, built in the 1920s, was made up of 93 buildings. Once the world's largest manufacturing complex, the plant had its own steel mill, Rouge Steel. The plant is on the Rouge River, a tributary of the Detroit River.

(GLEAM) Project published a list of the 13 most serious environmental stressors, out of 50, with which the Great Lakes are challenged:

- *Invasive mussels*
- *Climate, warming temperatures*
- *Invasion risk via ballast water*
"- *Invasive lamprey*
- *Invasive fish [such as the round goby and Asian carp]*
- *Climate, changing water levels*
- *Toxic metals, biomagnifying*
- *Decline of Diporeia [A small shrimp-like animal and major food source for commercially important fish species like lake whitefish and other fish that salmon, trout, and walleye eat.]*
- *Toxic organics, biomagnifying*
- *Non-point pollution [particularly phosphorus, which contributes to toxic algae blooms]*
- *Coastal development*
- *Non-point sediment*
- *Nuisance harmful algal blooms"*

Four of the top five concerns involve invasive species. Invasive species are non-native species whose populations native predators cannot control and whose presence is likely to cause environmental or economic harm. Invasive species often arrive in the ballast water tanks of ocean freighters. International shipping brought invasive species to the Great Lakes. Over 180 non-native species now live in the Great Lakes, and the first one that appeared still presents a major problem.

A sea lamprey is an ancient, jawless, parasitic fish, sometimes mistaken for an eel. With a large round mouth acting like a suction cup, a lamprey is able attach onto another fish. Its mouth is filled with sharp, curved teeth and a rough, scraping tongue. Sea lampreys live by sucking the blood of the fish to which they attach themselves. Sea lampreys were responsible for almost exterminating the lake trout, once the most desirable catch in the lakes.

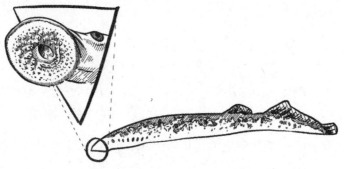

The sea lamprey was the first of many invasive species that came to the Great Lakes. It was first discovered in Lake Ontario in the 1830s.

Some invasive species have caused little or no harm in the Great Lakes. Others, like the sea lamprey, quagga and zebra mussels, and round goby, have upset the balance of native species in the lakes.

An invasive species causing new concern is the Asian carp, a relative of goldfish. Asian carp were brought to the southeastern US in the 1970s to control weeds and parasites in aquatic farms. Some escaped and spread up the Mississippi River system. These aggressive carp can grow up to four feet in length and weigh over 100 pounds. They have crowded out native fish species. Given the carp's size and large numbers, their waste has decreased the quality of the water. The resulting poor water quality has killed off sensitive species like freshwater mussels.

Asian carp lay hundreds of thousands of eggs at a time. They also easily spread into new areas, being able to jump barriers like low dams. A complex underwater electric fence of three barriers was constructed in the Sanitary and Ship Canal between the Mississippi River and Lake Michigan to keep them out of the Great Lakes. In both 2010 and 2017, one Asian carp was found beyond the electrified barrier, just miles from Lake Michigan.

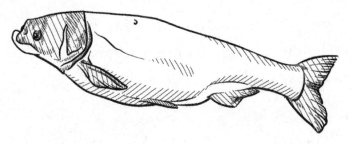

In the summer of 2017, an Asian carp was found beyond the electric barrier meant to keep Asian carp out of Lake Michigan and the rest of the Great Lakes.

Modern agriculture has negatively impacted the Great Lakes, too. Farmers apply fertilizers and pesticides to their fields. When the fertilizers run off into the lakes, especially shallow Lake Erie, algae feed on the nutrients meant for farm crops. This makes the algae grow very quickly in thick scums that discolor the water. Some of these algae blooms produce neurotoxins, liver toxins, and skin irritants. These toxins harm wildlife, swimmers, waders, and pets.

These toxins have even contaminated drinking water. In 2014, a large algae bloom on Lake Erie caused a two-day ban on tap water in Toledo, Ohio for over 400,000 residents. The toxins in the tap water exceeded the World Health Organization's level for safe drinking water. This one algae bloom is estimated to have cost $65 million in terms of its negative effects on water-related activities and human health.

A massive algae bloom in the Western Basin of Lake Erie contaminated drinking water and kept people and pets from enjoying the lake as it floated towards shore.

With drought becoming a problem in the southwestern United States, the world's increasing need for fresh water has come closer to the Great Lakes. In 1998, an Ontario company planned to export over 158 million gallons of Lake Superior water annually to Asia on tanker ships. The Ontario Ministry of the Environment initially approved this plan. Once the news spread, politicians and residents on both sides of the border were angry and took action.

To avoid such a plan from ever becoming reality, the Great Lakes Compact was created. It bans the diversion of Great Lakes water outside the basin, with limited exceptions. Great Lakes water is used to brew beer in Milwaukee and to make soda pop in Michigan.

Scientists believe climate change is responsible for increasing temperatures, causing extreme weather, harming ecosystems, and raising sea levels. Climate change could affect the Great Lakes in several ways. Rising temperatures could lower water levels in the lakes, intensify harmful algae blooms, and threaten fish and wildlife. Climate change, in affecting temperature and precipitation, causes extreme weather, which can affect water quality, ice coverage, shipping, tourism, and recreation.

A National Oceanic and Atmospheric Administration (NOAA) scientific team, the Great Lakes Integrated Sciences and Assessments (GLISA) has found the average air temperature in the Great Lakes region has risen by two degrees since 1900. However, the Great Lakes' waters have warmed twice as fast as the surrounding air since 1980.

Since 1995, average surface water temperatures have increased slightly for each of the Great Lakes. The onset of the first ice cover on inland lakes is 6 to 11 days later than in the mid-nineteenth century. The breakup of ice cover in the spring is 2 to 13 days earlier. This shorter winter and open-lake waters occurring earlier in the spring are causing the lakes to warm for longer periods of time. According to research by GLISA, this increases the effects of warmer summer air temperatures. The frequency and intensity of storms, floods, and heat waves in the Great Lakes region are expected to continue to increase.

Regulations and laws are protecting the Great Lakes from worsening industrial pollution or greater water diversion. Invasive species, agricultural run-off, and climate change remain tremendous challenges. Will we solve them quickly enough to save our Great Lakes?

Climate change means more extreme weather on the Great Lakes.

Chapter 9
The Great Lakes as Magnet

How happy the descendants of those early humans who first crossed the Bering Land Bridge must have been to discover the Great Lakes! Native Americans remained in the region because the lakes provided easy access to food, clothing, and shelter. Today, including the Native Americans and First Nations people living on and off reservations and reserves, an estimated 33 million people live in the Great Lakes Basin.

Having provided life's essentials to Native Americans, what else has drawn people to the Great Lakes? In the ninetenth and twentieth centuries, employment opportunities brought Americans, Canadians, and European immigrants to the Basin. The majority of people on the US side live in urban areas around the ten industrial cities on shores of the Great Lakes. The basin also includes eight of Canada's 20 largest cities: Toronto, Hamilton, London, St. Catharines, Niagara, Oshawa, Windsor, and Barrie. The natural resources in the Great Lakes Basin determined what industries developed. The industries in the area were often responsible for the growth of these cities. Today, two major industries in the region are mining and energy.

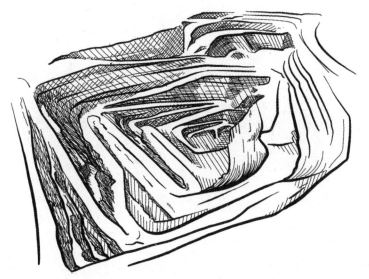

Tilden Mine is one of two iron mines in the Upper Peninsula of Michigan. Together the two mines produce 20% of North America's iron ore.

Many mines are located in Ontario, Minnesota, Wisconsin, and Michigan. The main mining resources here are still heavy metals, especially iron and copper.

The mining of frac sand is also becoming more important in the region as fracking gains prevalence on the continent. Frac sand is high-purity quartz sand with very durable round grains. It is used in the fracking process to extract oil and natural gas from rock.

A windfarm on Wolfe Island has 86 wind turbines which take advantage of offshore winds to produce energy.

Thirty-eight nuclear power plants dot the Great Lakes Basin. Wind turbines are going up around the lakes and on some of their islands to take advantage of the offshore wind power. Some conservationists are concerned about the turbines impact on migratory birds and bats.

Many people who live near a Great Lake earn their living in an industry associated with the lakes, such as shipping or tourism. Many tourists visit the Great Lakes. What do these Great Lakes tourists find to do?

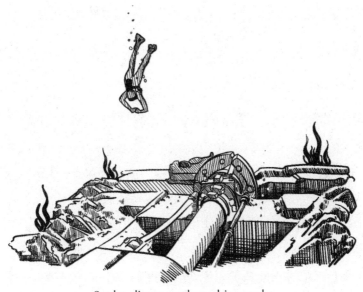

Scuba divers explore shipwrecks
near Chicago in Lake Michigan.

Many people are interested in what is under the the surface of the water and go fishing or dive to shipwrecks.

Others spend time on the water's surface in kayaks, canoes, sailboats, or motorboats. Some spend time directly on the water, water-skiing, jet-skiing, windsurfing, or parasailing. Occasionally, a surfer on a traditional surfboard, more likely to be skimming ocean waves, is spotted.

Cruise lines offer lake cruises, but no one has to spend a lot of money to get out in the middle of the Great Lakes. In 2016, at least 136 of the more than 35,000 Great Lakes Basin islands were accessible by ferry or bridge.

One of the best ways to get to know a Great Lake is by visiting a national lakeshore or a national park on a lakeshore. The United States protects four such coastal areas, preserved by the US Congress for their special natural and recreational value, and operated by the National Park Service. All of these national costal areas offer campgrounds and showcase historic preservation and scientific research projects. All three national lakeshores are in the Great Lakes Basin: Apostle Islands National Lakeshore in Wisconsin, Pictured Rocks National Lakeshore and Sleeping Bear Dunes National Lakeshore, both in Michigan.

The fourth nationally protected Great Lakes coastal area was the Indiana Dunes National Lakeshore in Indiana. In 2019 it became the 61st national park and was renamed the Indiana Dunes National Park. It is known for sand beaches, small dunes, and forests along fifteen miles of the southern shore of Lake Michigan.

Visitors can kayak in the sea caves of Apostle Islands National Lakeshore on Lake Superior.

The Apostle Islands National Lakeshore includes 21 of Lake Superior's Apostle Islands plus 12 miles of mainland shoreline. Among other features, the islands are known for eight historic lighthouses. Several old-growth remnant forests and a number of natural habitats for birds, mammals, plants, amphibians, and aquatic species are found on the islands as well. Wildlife there include black bear, whitetail deer, snowshoe hare, red fox, coyote, beaver, and otter.

Visitors hike the islands and often travel by kayak between them and into sea caves. Scuba divers visit the sea caves, too, as well as area shipwrecks. Many people come to fish. Northland College Apostle Island School is an outdoor environmental residential program for middle-school students.

Pictured Rocks National Lakeshore features 15 miles of magnificent sandstone cliffs, 12 miles of beaches, and five miles of enormous sand dunes on Lake Superior. Waterfalls, sea caves, lighthouses, and shipwrecks are other attractions. Almost 100 miles of trails wind through the 42 miles of shoreline.

Sleeping Bear Dunes National Lakeshore features 400-foot-high sand dunes, the two Manitou Islands, and 65 miles of sandy beach, forest, and farms on the eastern shore of Lake Michigan. Visitors hike and climb, paddle and swim, and explore museums and towns.

Visitors can find much more to do on a Great Lakes beach than just swim, sun, or stroll. Treasure can be found on land, not just in shipwrecks. As on ocean shores, beachgoers can find driftwood polished into fantastical shapes. With the help of metal detectors, valuable historic treasures are found under the sand. A glint of color in the sand may signal a piece of beach glass. While clear glass and shades of green and brown are the most common, collectors hoard blue glass and occasionally find lavender, yellow, or red.

However, on Great Lakes beaches, many strollers are hunting for something that cannot be found at an ocean: Petoskey stones! The Petoskey stone has been Michigan's state stone since 1965. The stone is named after the Michigan city of Petoskey, but to find one, you don't have to be in Petoskey.

A Petoskey stone is not actually a stone. It is the fossil of an extinct coral called "Hexagonaria pericarnata." This marine animal lived in colonies in warm, shallow, saltwater seas. This gray fossil is identified by its hexagonal segments arranged in a honeycomb pattern. These segments become easier to see when the fossil is wet, as do the "eyes" in the center of the hexagons.

Although some people claim Petoskey stones are only found on the northern Lower Peninsula shorelines of Lake Michigan-Huron, they have been found on southern shores, in Indiana and Illinois, and at Lake Erie and Lake Ontario. Many specimens have been rounded and polished smooth by running glacial water or lake waves. Many other kinds of fossils are also found on the shores of the Great Lakes.

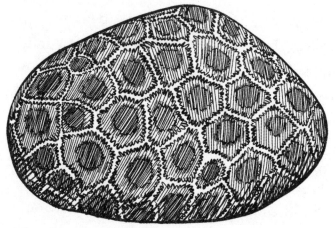

A Petoskey stone is the fossil of a coral that lived in warm shallow seas 350 million years ago.

Lake Superior is not a good place to find Petoskey stones, but Lake Superior offers a special prize for rockhounds: Lake Superior agates. The Lake Superior agate has been Minnesota's state gem since 1969. Agates are colorful banded rocks that are classified as semi-precious gemstones. Lake Superior agates are primarily red, orange, and yellow. These colors are caused by iron leaching from rocks, oxidizing, and staining chalcedony, a type of quartz. These agates were formed during the lava eruptions that occurred a billion years ago.

On state-owned land in Michigan, it is illegal to remove more than 25 pounds of rock, mineral, or fossil. In 2015, a Michigan man removed a 93-pound Petoskey stone from Lake Michigan near Northport. This huge Petoskey stone was confiscated and is now displayed at the DNR Outdoor Adventure Center in Detroit. This center's slogan is "Up North, Downtown" and it is a great place to visit when one does not have the opportunity to head Up North, which in "Michigan's mitten" usually involves visiting a Great Lake.

But, why not aim to experience the real thing? Imagine what might attract a visitor to the Great Lakes. All five Great Lakes—with a total of 9,577 miles of shoreline stretching through eight states and one province—await exploration and promise adventure, from diving to the depths of a shipwreck to climbing to the heights of a towering sand dune, with lots of fun in between!

Select Quotes about the Great Lakes

"As fine a land as it is possible to see"

> —Jacques Cartier, French explorer, 1534

"This waterway, linking the oceans of the world with the Great Lakes of the American continent, is the culmination of the dreams of thousands of individuals on both sides of our common Canadian-United States border. . . . The St. Lawrence Seaway presents to the world a 2300-mile waterway of locks, lakes, and man-made channels. . . . We pause to salute all those who have shared in this task, from the architects and the planners to the artisans and the workers who have spent countless hours in its construction."

> —President Dwight Eisenhower at the formal opening of the St. Lawrence Seaway, June 26, 1959

"Those dunes are to the Midwest what the Grand Canyon is to Arizona and the Yosemite to California. They constitute a signature of time and eternity . . . once lost, the loss would be irrevocable."

> —Carl Sandburg, American poet, 1958

"I do not think the measure of a civilization is how tall its buildings of concrete are, but rather how well its people have learned to relate to their environment and fellow [humans]."

> —Sun Bear, an actor, author, and medicine man of Ojibwe descent

Glossary

Algae bloom A rapid increase in algae population, often a result of fertilizer that runs into the water.

Archipelago A group of islands.

Bering Land Bridge The land between Siberia and Alaska that appeared when sea levels dropped during the last ice age. It is likely that Paleo-Indians used this "bridge," to cross from Asia to North America around 12,000–10,500 BC.

Delta A flat piece of land, often triangular in shape, which splits a river into multiple strands at its mouth.

First Nations People The term used in Canada for native people.

Fracking Use of liquids under pressure to break rocks below the earth's surface to extract natural gas or oil.

Invasive species A non-native species which presents a likely risk of environmental or economic harm.

Laurentian River System An ancient river system that later became four of the five Great Lakes.

Laurentide Ice Sheet The glaciers that covered North America for five million years.

Manoomin Ojibwe name for a high protein, low-fat grain that grows in water in the northern Great Lakes region. It is an Ojibwe diet staple and has spiritual significance.

Midcontinent Rift A 950-mile fracture in the continent, running from what is now Kansas to Lake Superior, the volcanic activity of which created Lake Superior's basin.

New France The land in North America claimed by France beginning in 1534.

Non-point pollution Water or air pollution not occurring from one identifiable source.

Nonrenewable resource A natural resource that is destroyed in its use.

Paleo-Indians Early humans who most likely crossed the Bering Land Bridge to North America and were the first people to live in the Great Lakes region. They became extinct 9,000 years ago.

Paleozoic Era A time period on Earth between 570 million and 230 million years ago. Fish, insects, and reptiles evolved. Shallow, warm, saltwater seas covered what would become the Great Lakes region.

Peninsula An outcrop of land surrounded on three sides by water

Pleistocene Epoch A time period on Earth that occured between 2 million years ago and 10,000 years ago when the earth was in its latest ice age and modern humans evolved.

Pre-Columbian cultures The native cultures who evolved from the Paleo-Indians and lived in North America before Christopher Columbus approached its southeastern shores.

Precambrian Era The earliest of the earth's four eras, which ended 570 million years ago and during which the earth's crust formed.

Renewable resource A natural resource that is not destroyed in its use.

St. Lawrence Power Project A part of the St. Lawrence Seaway involving three dams, which control the water levels to provide a dependable flow of water to generate hydropower.

St. Lawrence Seaway A joint project between the United States and Canada that made it possible to navigate from the Great Lakes to the Atlantic Ocean.

Strait A narrow body of water between two peninsulas that connects two bodies of water.

Wisconsin Glacial Stage The most recent cycle of the earth cooling and glaciers expanding, which ended about 10,000 years ago.

Wind turbines Built to process wind into mechanical power, which can be converted to electricity.

Great Lakes Timeline

1 billion BCE Midcontinent Rift allows volcanic activity to erupt from core of earth, forming Lake Superior's basin.

350 million BCE Warm shallow seas cover the area that will someday contain the Great Lakes.

5 million BCE Glaciers advance and retreat.

18,000 BCE Glacial grooves are gouged by the movement of the glaciers into what will become the bedrock of four of the five Great Lakes.

11,000 BCE The Great Lakes form over 3,000 years of the last stage of the most recent ice age.

6,000 BCE Native people establish hunting and fishing communities throughout the Great Lakes region.

1490 The Anishinaabe end their 500-year Seven Fires Migration to and across the Great Lakes region.

1534 June 9 Jacques Cartier is the first European to discover the St. Lawrence River and claim land, which would become part of New France.

1679 *Le Griffon* is the first full-size sailing vessel on the Great Lakes, also, most likely, the first shipwreck.

1763 The French and Indian War ends with the Paris Treaty of 1763, giving the Great Lakes region to Great Britain.

1797 The first lock in the Great Lakes Basin is constructed.

1825 October 26 The Erie Canal opens, connecting the Great Lakes to the Atlantic Ocean.

1829 November The Welland Canal opens, connecting Lake Erie and Lake Ontario in Canada, resolving the 326-foot difference in elevation between the two lakes.

World Timeline

1.6 billion BCE First blue-green algae (cyanobacteria) appear on earth. It is the first organism with the ability to create oxygen via photosynthesis.

650 million BCE First animals appear on Earth, in the ocean.

250,000 BCE First humans (*Homo sapiens*) appear on the earth.

12,000 BCE Paleo-Indians, the first human inhabitants of North America come from Asia, possibly crossing the Bering Land Bridge.

1000 Viking explorer Leif Ericson sails from Iceland to North America, landing on what he names Vinland (later to be called Newfoundland).

1453 May 29 Constantinople is captured, cutting off the Silk Road, the European trading route by land to China, India, and the Southeastern Asian islands.

1492 Christopher Columbus crosses the Atlantic Ocean, looking for a northwest passage.

1497 Giovanni Caboto, aka John Cabot, is the first European since the Vikings to reach North America, landing on Newfoundland and claiming it for England.

1775–1783 American Revolutionary War.

1861–1865 American Civil War.

1903–1906 Norwegian Explorer Roald Amundsen is the first person to navigate the long-sought Northwest Passage between the Atlantic and Pacific Oceans.

Great Lakes Timeline (cont.)

1830s The sea lamprey, a parasitic invasive species, is first observed in Lake Ontario. Within 100 years, it is found in all of the Great Lakes.

1855 The Soo Locks first opens, making Lake Superior accessible to the rest of the Great Lakes region for shipping.

1908 June 29 Great Lakes Pirate "Roaring" Dan Seavey is arrested.

1959 April 15 The St. Lawrence Seaway opens to allow ocean-going vessels to sail between the Great Lakes and the Atlantic Ocean.

1969 June 22 An oil slick on the polluted Cuyahoga River catches fire, prompting a number of water pollution control measures be put in place.

1975 November The SS Edmund Fitzgerald leaves Superior, Wisconsin and sinks in Lake Superior with no survivors during a storm.

2008 December 8 The Great Lakes Compact is signed into law, banning the diversion of Great Lakes water outside of the Great Lakes Basin.

2014 August 2 Toledo bans residents from drinking city water from Lake Erie after tests confirm unsafe levels of the algal toxin Microcystin.

2017 June 22 An invasive Asian carp is found just nine miles from Lake Michigan.

World Timeline (cont.)

1917–1918 The US participates in World War I.

1941–1945 The US participates in World War II.

1969 July 20 The United States lands Apollo 11 on the moon, where Neil Armstrong and Buzz Aldrin are the first humans to walk on the moon.

2001 September 11 Also known as 9/11, the United States is hit by four terrorist attacks by the terrorist group al-Qaeda.

2008 November 4 Barack Obama is elected the first African-American president of the United States.

2016 April 16–2017 June 1 Standing Rock Resistance is led by 10,000 Native Americans resisting the construction of the Dakota Access Pipeline.

Bibliography

Berton, Pierre. *The Great Lakes*. Toronto: Stoddart Publishing Co. Ltd., 1996.

Dennis, Jerry. *The Living Great Lakes: Searching for the Heart of the Inland Seas*. New York: Thomas Dunne Books-St. Martin's Press, 2003.

Dunphy, Maureen. *Great Lakes Island Escapes: Ferries and Bridges to Adventure*. Detroit: Painted Turtle-Wayne State University Press, 2016.

Grady, Wayne. *The Great Lakes: The Natural History of a Changing Region*. Vancouver: Greystone Books, 2007.

Havighurst, Walter, ed. *The Great Lakes Reader*. New York: Collier Books-Macmillan Publishing Co. Inc., 1966.

Rapia, William. *Lake Invaders: Invasive Species and the Battle for the Future of the Great Lakes*. Detroit: Wayne State University Press, 2016.

Smith, Sigrid D. P., et al. "Rating impacts in a multi-stressor world: a quantitative assessment of 50 stressors affecting the Great Lakes." *Ecological Applications*, Vol. 25, No. 3 April, 2015, pp. 717 – 728. Deep Blue University of Michigan Library. Accessed Web 6 Feb. 2018.

Further Reading

Benton-Banai, Edward. *The Mishomis Book; The Voice of the Ojibway*. Minneapolis: University of Minnesota Press, 2010.

Butts, Ed. *Shipwrecks, Monsters and Mysteries of the Great Lakes*. Toronto: Tundra Books, 2011.

Holling, Clancy Holling. *Paddle-to-the-Sea*. Boston: HMH Books for Young Readers, 1941.

Hatcher, Harlan and Erich A Walter. *A Pictorial History of the Great Lakes*. New York: Bonanza Books

Kantar, Andrew. *29 Missing: The True and Tragic Story of the Disappearance of the SS Edmund Fitzgerald*. Lansing: Michigan State University Press, 1998.

For Online Exploration

Teach Great Lakes: Great Lakes Region Educational Blog. http://teachgreatlakes.net/

Teaching Great Lakes Science: Lessons & Data Sets. http://www.miseagrant.umich.edu/lessons/

Index

Index (cont.)

Index (cont.)

Index (cont.)

Index (cont.)

Index (cont.)

About the Author

Writer **Maureen Dunphy** has lived her entire life on Michigan's lower peninsula and loves that she can easily find her special state on any map—even in photos from space—by looking for the "mitten" peninsula surrounded by the blue of the Great Lakes.

Dunphy enjoys spending time at her cottage on Pelee Island, a Canadian island in Lake Erie. Over two summers, Maureen Dunphy planned and took 27 trips to a total of 135 other Great Lakes Basin islands that are accessible by bridge or ferry. She wrote a book about her Great Lakes island adventures entitled *Great Lakes Island Escapes: Ferries and Bridges to Adventure*, published in 2016.

When she's not writing, one of her very favorite pastimes is walking the shoreline of Pelee Island looking for the rare Petoskey stone and the many other limestone fossils Lake Erie tumbles ashore.

All About... Series

A series for inquisitive young readers

If you liked this book, you may also enjoy:

- All About Winston Churchill
- All About Roberto Clemente
- All About Frederick Douglass
- All About Amelia Earhart
- All About the Grand Canyon
- All About Benjamin Franklin
- All About Stephen Hawking
- All About Sir Edmund Hillary
- All About Helen Keller
- All About Martin Luther King, Jr.
- All About Julia Morgan
- All About Madam C. J. Walker
- All About Steve Wozniak
- All About Yellowstone
- All About the Appalachian Trail
- All About Mohandas Gandhi
- All About Barack Obama

Visit brpressbooks.com for free teachers' guides, games, and puzzles.